Grade 5 Piano Solos
16 enjoyable pieces for Grade 5 p

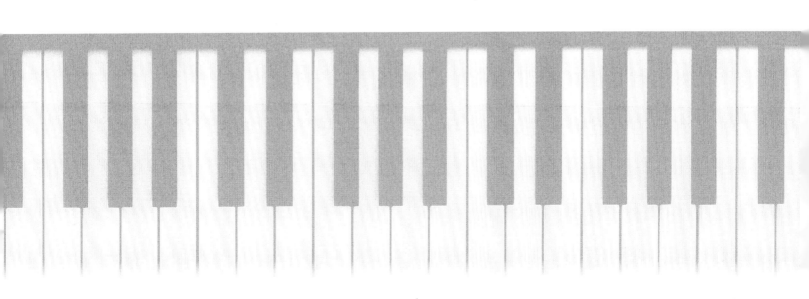

Published by
Chester Music

Exclusive Distributors:
Hal Leonard
7777 West Bluemound Road
Milwaukee, WI 53213
Email: info@halleonard.com

Hal Leonard Europe Limited
42 Wigmore Street
Marylebone, London, W1U 2RN
Email: info@halleonardeurope.com

Hal Leonard Australia Pty. Ltd.
4 Lentara Court
Cheltenham, Victoria, 3192 Australia
Email: info@halleonard.com.au

Order No. CH83666
ISBN 978-1-78305-976-8
This book © Copyright 2015 Chester Music Limited.
All Rights Reserved.

Edited by Toby Knowles.
Arranged by Alistair Watson.
Music processed by Paul Ewers Music Design.

Printed in the EU.

Grade 5 Piano Solos

16 enjoyable pieces for Grade 5 pianists

CHESTER MUSIC

Contents

Bridge Over Troubled Water

Words & Music by Paul Simon

There are some big stretches in the right-hand chords. Try to keep the top line legato throughout.
This song is fairly quiet and subdued, but it builds to a loud finish.

Cantaloupe Island

Music by Herbie Hancock

Enjoy the rhythms and bluesy chords in this jazz standard.

Don't use pedal—it will be much more effective if the playing is dry, especially in the piano solo (from bar 22).

To Coda ⊕

D.S. al Coda   ⊕ Coda

Flower Duet (from *Lakmé*)

Leo Delibes

Practise the right-hand thirds before starting the whole piece—it will be a good warm-up.

The left hand has some tricky leaps, but they don't always need to be legato—follow the slurs as they are marked in the music.

Above all, try to capture the beauty of this piece.

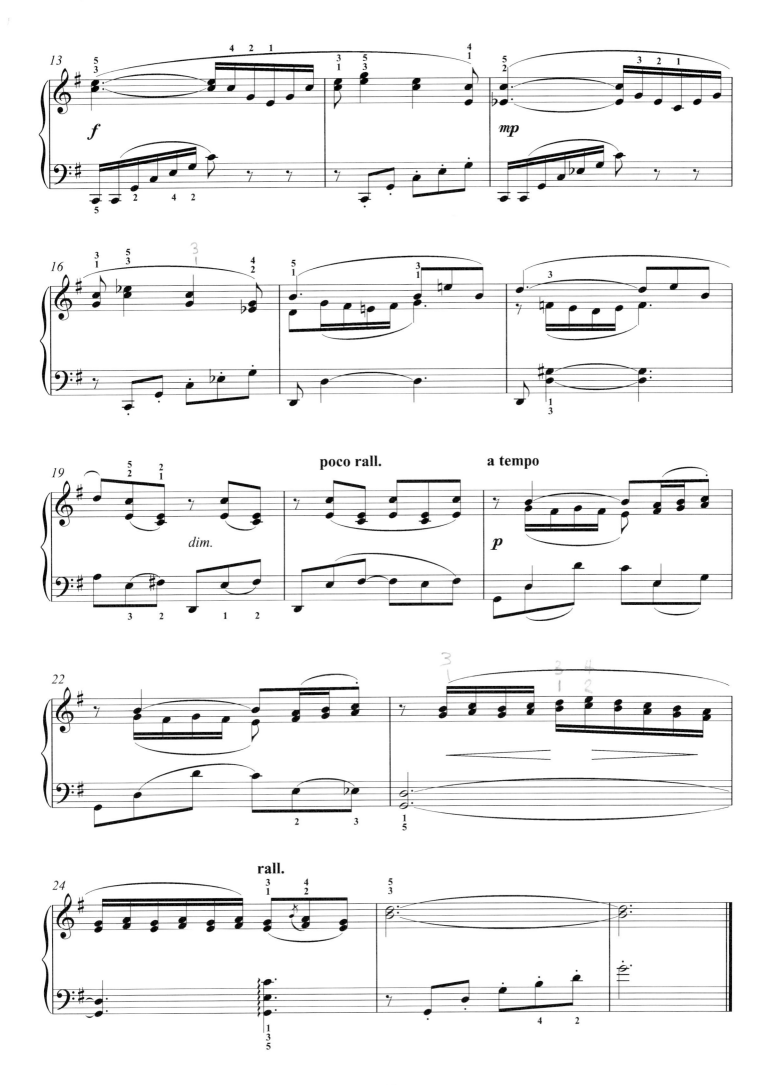

For The Love Of A Princess
(from *Braveheart*)

Music by by James Horner

Take plenty of time to let the music breathe, and watch out for the changes of time signature.
Explore the full range of dynamics, from *pp* to *ff*.

Freely (♩ = 48)

Gymnopédie No. I

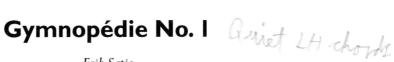

Erik Satie

Try to capture the dreamlike atmosphere in this piece. You will need to use the pedal to ensure the bass note sounds throughout each bar. There are several bars in which the right hand needs to play the top note of the chord.

Adagio ($\mathbf{\downarrow = 76}$)

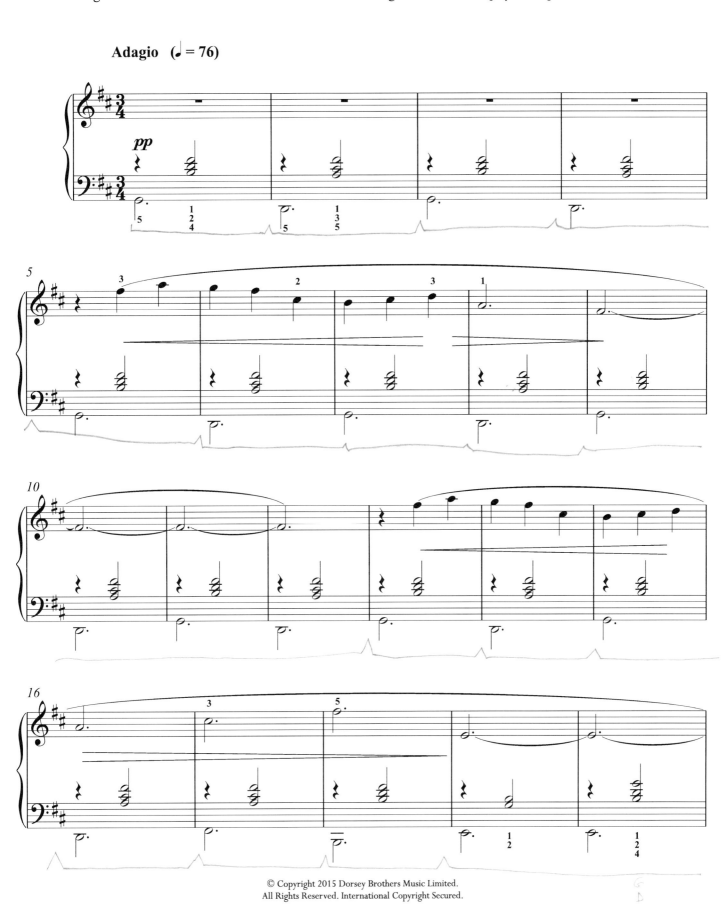

Kiss The Rain

Music by Yiruma & Min Seok Kim

This piece should be played very softly and delicately.
There are some big stretches in the left hand—using the pedal will help with this.

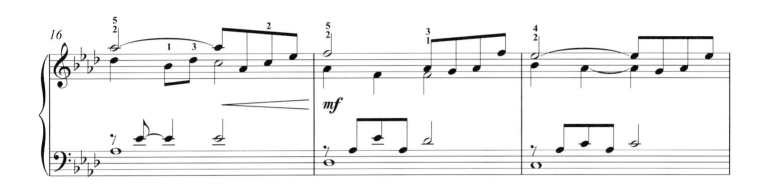

D.S. al Coda

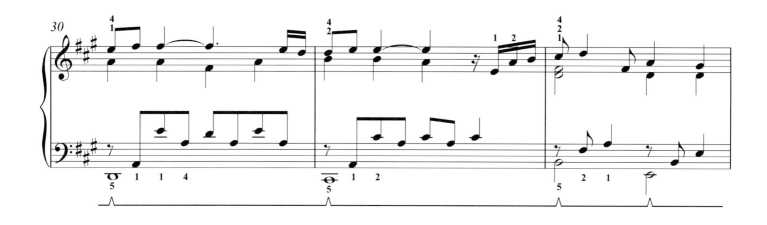

Waltz No. 3, Op. 39

Johannes Brahms

This piece has a sweet and slightly melancholy mood.
The right-hand melody should be played cantabile, and the left hand very light.

Maple Leaf Rag

Scott Joplin

This piece should be happy and playful. Make the most of the syncopations in the right hand and keep the left hand detached. Don't try to play too fast—ragtime should never be very fast.

Mas Que Nada (Say No More)

Words & Music by Jorge Ben

Enjoy the latin rhythms in this piece. The right hand is very syncopated, but the left hand is rhythmically very straightforward.

Rondo Alla Turca

Wolfgang Amadeus Mozart

There is quite a lot of semiquaver detail in this piece. Try to play evenly in the scale passages and choose an achievable tempo. The left-hand rolled chords should sound like a flourish. Use some pedal for these.

Allegretto (♩ = 122)

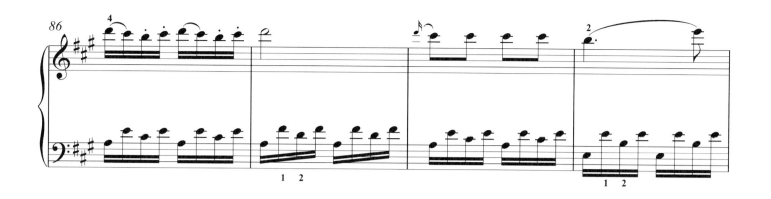

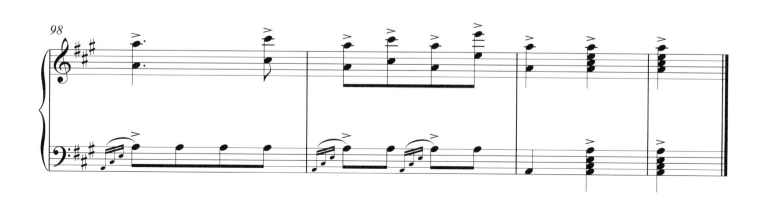

Prelude in A Major, Op.28

Frédéric Chopin

In this pretty miniature you can work on phrasing and dynamic control.
Take a little time at the climax in bar 12, and observe the comma (pause) which follows.

Prelude in C Minor, Op. 28

Frédéric Chopin

Aim for a full, rich fortissimo that's never harsh. Bring out the change in colour from bar 5 and see if you can bring it right down to pianissimo towards the end. There are a few chords where the right-hand thumb needs to play two notes.

Take Five

Music by Paul Desmond

This is fast and rhythmic. As long as you get the sense of the swing rhythm, the 5/4 metre should take care of itself.
A gentle wrist rotation will help with the blue notes in bar 5.

Träumerei

Robert Schumann

This piece has many interweaving strands of melody. Try to let each line come through the texture.
Make sure you let the music breathe, and place each rolled chord carefully.

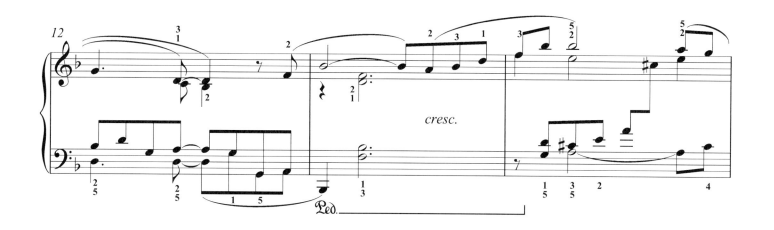

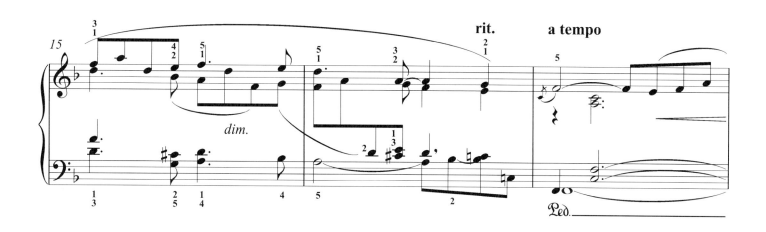

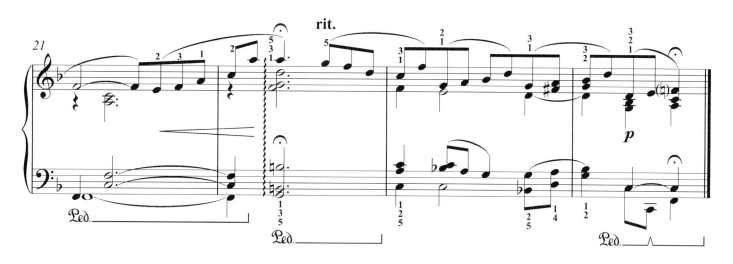

Una Mattina

Ludovico Einaudi

This piece needs plenty of pedal, but only subtle light and shade—the dynamics are fairly consistent.
Let the notes weave in and out, creating a dreamlike atmosphere.

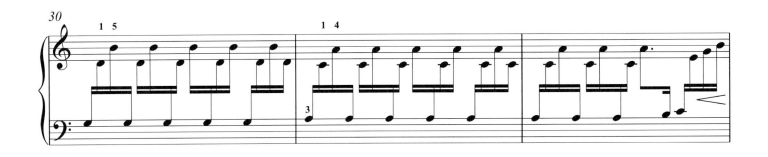

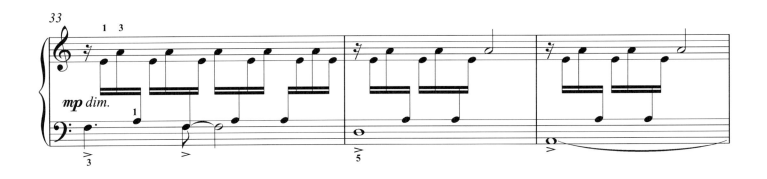

Your Song

Words & Music by Elton John & Bernie Taupin

Play this in a relaxed manner, with light semiquavers in each hand.

Graded Piano Solos

The 16 pieces in these books have been specially arranged to provide enjoyable supplementary repertoire for pianists. Each piece has been adapted to fit within the specifications of the major exam board grades, and each book covers a wide range of styles, from classical and jazz pieces to contemporary pop.

Grade 1 Piano Solos

Including:
Amazing Grace; Lean On Me;
Do You Want To Build A Snowman?

CH83622

Grade 2 Piano Solos

Including:
All Of Me; Eine Kleine
Nachtmusik; Let It Go

CH83633

Grade 3 Piano Solos

Including:
Für Elise; The Snow Prelude No. 3;
Someone Like You

CH83644

Grade 4 Piano Solos

Including:
Air On The G String; Make You
Feel My Love; Summertime

CH83655

Grade 5 Piano Solos

Including:
Bridge Over Troubled Water;
Una Mattina; Take Five

CH83666